PREFACE

There has been a broad and dramatic trend towards liberalisation of trade and investment policies in non-OECD economies in recent decades. However, financial crises that have erupted in East Asia, Russia and Brazil over the last two years have shaken the global economy. Concerns have been expressed that countries suffering from financial crises might turn away from open trade and investment -- even though they have been the motor of economic growth and poverty reduction. And widening current account imbalances in the OECD area have raised the risks of protectionist pressures.

This report reviews some of the evidence on the benefits and challenges of trade and investment for development, drawing on some experiences of a number of economies in various parts of the world. These experiences show that trade and investment have been beneficial for development, when accompanied by a coherent set of growth-oriented macroeconomic and structural policies, capacity-building, adequate social policy and good governance. Further, in response to financial crises in recent years, both Korea and Mexico have continued with liberalisation and structural reforms. These policies are helping Korea, like Mexico before it, to recover and establish a sounder base for future economic development.

Today's globalising world economy generates a coincidence of interests for all countries in building strong policies and institutions for a well-functioning market economy, and moving ahead with more open trade and investment. Strong trade and investment partners are necessary to achieve increased prosperity, greater political security and improved environmental management in the 21st century.

In this context, all countries share strong interests in a new WTO round of multilateral trade negotiations. Such a round must be responsive to the needs of developing and transition economies, to ensure that they can reap the full benefits for development of integration into the world economy.

This publication is published under the authority of the Secretary-General, and makes available to a wider audience results of OECD work in order to help inform public debate in this important area. It follows up the 1998 OECD report "Open Markets Matter", which discusses the benefits of trade and investment for people in OECD countries and the world more generally. Under the direction of Deputy Secretary-General Kumiharu Shigehara, the principal author was John West of the Secretary-General's Private Office. Significant contributions were made by Randall Jones and Benedicte Larre (Economics Department), Tom Jones (Environment Directorate), Richard Carey (Development Co-operation Directorate), Crawford Falconer, Blanka Kalinova and Raed Safadi (Trade Directorate), Steve Thomsen (Directorate for Financial, Fiscal and Enterprise Affairs) and Ulrich Hiemenz (Development Centre).

A companion publication to this volume, entitled "Policy Coherence Matters", addresses the foundations of market-oriented development, in terms of policies, capacities and good governance, and the responsibilities which OECD countries have to systematically consider concerning the effects of their own policies on the developing economies.

TABLE OF CONTENTS

5

EXECUTIVE SUMMARY

Financial crises have brought risks of protectionism

Liberalisation of trade and investment by non-OECD economies has been a dominant trend in the global economy in recent decades. However, concerns have been expressed that countries suffering from financial crises might turn away from open trade and investment. And widening current account imbalances in the OECD area have raised the risk of protectionist pressures.

This report reviews evidence of the benefits and challenges of trade and investment liberalisation for development. Although this is a longstanding issue on the international agenda, it has come into sharper focus, looking ahead to the Third WTO Ministerial Meeting in Seattle and to the launching of a broad-based Round of trade negotiations.

The conclusion of this report is that open trade and investment have been beneficial for development when accompanied by a coherent set of growth-oriented macroeconomic and structural policies, capacity-building, adequate social policy and good governance. Further, countries that have responded to economic crisis with liberalisation and structural reform have experienced positive results. In this regard, all countries have an interest in pushing ahead with more open trade and investment, and in building strong policies and institutions for a well-functioning market economy.

Trends in liberalisation

Liberalisation of trade and investment has been a driving force in the rapid economic development of OECD countries in the post-war period. Following in their footsteps, many developing and then transition economies started abandoning state-led, inward-oriented strategies adopted in the post-War period, and are now active participants in world trade and investment.

... but
liberalisation
continues in
response to
financial crisis

Over the last two years with financial crises in East Asia, Russia and then Brazil, there has not been a general rise in protectionism. On the contrary. Most crisis-affected countries are continuing to liberalise trade and investment, which they see as the solution to the crisis, not the cause.

Liberalisation of trade and investment has been implemented autonomously, in regional integration arrangements and in multilateral negotiations. Multilateral liberalisation offers many additional benefits:

- Domestic public support can be enhanced when liberalisation is part of a global effort in which all countries make substantial contributions.

- Benefits can be greater when a country's liberalisation is accompanied by liberalisation by others; and

- Transparent and binding rules-based liberalisation provides insurance against protectionist pressures, and can add credibility to individual countries' liberalisation efforts.

OECD
countries need
to show
leadership in
advancing
multilateral
liberalisation

While developing countries generally support trade and investment liberalisation, some still have reservations about a new Round trade negotiations, which they fear will be dominated by concerns of developed countries. OECD countries need to show leadership in ensuring that the interests of all countries – developed, developing and transition economies – are taken into account. In this regard, OECD countries have a responsibility to consider the effect of their policies on developing and transition economies, especially regarding market access. It is also important to support capacity-building in developing countries, and to accord particular priority to supporting growth in least developed countries.

Benefits and challenges of open trade and investment for development

Open trade and investment is beneficial for economic development ...

Economies with open trade and investment can: (i) specialise in what they are best at; (ii) create competitive industries, (iii) stimulate domestic and foreign investment, (iv) exploit economies of scale and (v) benefit from transfers of knowledge, technology and organisational capacities, through access to new products and processes.

Empirical evidence confirms that the record of growth and poverty reduction achieved by developing countries which have liberalised trade and investment stands as one of the more remarkable episodes in the history of economic development. In particular:

- Open economies have grown significantly faster than closed economies over sustained periods of time.

- With open trade and investment generating higher growth, the evidence is that this growth is also associated with reductions in poverty.

- Income levels of "open" developing economies have been converging towards those of developed countries, whereas income levels of closed economies have fallen even further behind.

- There has also been a positive association between successfully sustained trade and investment liberalisation and improvements in core labour standards.

- Open economies have been able take much greater advantage of skilled workforces than closed economies -- many high growth economies have had the combination of outward-oriented policies and high literacy rates.

... when it is part of a coherent set of policies and reforms ...

While the general conclusions are clear, the experiences of developing countries with open trade and investment are quite diverse. No country has perfectly open trade and investment regimes. Specific interventions have often been used: some with apparent success, and some with dramatic failure. And relative openness has generally been achieved progressively. The evidence suggests that to reap the full benefits of open trade and investment, it must be part of a coherent set of policies and reforms.

It goes without saying that developing countries are at various stages of development. And one-size policies won't fit all. Nevertheless, a minimum degree of policy success is necessary in the following areas in order to benefit from open trade and investment – macroeconomic stability; strong financial systems; sound public and corporate governance; human resource development; environmental management; and structural adjustment.

... as illustrated by experiences of Mexico, Korea and transition economies

Mexico, Korea, some transition economies and also many others, provide examples of the importance of combining trade and investment liberalisation, with a coherent set of reforms and policies. They also provide examples of countries which have adjusted successfully to economic crisis thanks to liberalisation and structural reform.

- The Mexican government reaffirmed its commitment to reform at the time of the 1994 financial crisis. Thanks to increased flexibility and strength, the Mexican economy rebounded quickly and strongly from the crisis of 1994/95, with GDP growth averaging 5 ½ per cent from 1996-98.

- Korea has been taking dramatic reform measures in response to its financial crisis, including by radically opening its capital account, racing well ahead of its accession-obligations under the OECD codes. It is already seeing signs of recovery, and GDP, which fell by 6 per cent in 1998, could grow by 6 ½ per cent in 1999.

- The resistance of individual transition economies to the effects of the financial crises in East Asia, Russia and Brazil has been directly linked to the success of the liberalisation efforts in diversifying their export markets and attracting durable investment flows.

International co-operation

Today's globalising world economy provides a co-incidence of interests for all countries ...

Today's globalising world economy generates a coincidence of interests for all countries -- in pushing ahead with more open trade and investment, and in building strong policies and institutions for a well-functioning market economy. Strong trade and investment partners are necessary to achieve increased prosperity, greater political security and improved environmental management in the 21st century.

All countries -- developed, developing and transition – are working together through the whole range of international institutions, including the OECD, to secure sustainable development and integrate successfully into the global economy. The OECD has a wide range of activities for policy dialogue between Members and non-members, particularly to facilitate their successful integration into the international economic system.

... in a new Round of multilateral negotiations

A priority issue is the preparation for a broad-based new Round of multilateral trade negotiations. All countries have a vital stake in a new Round to prepare for the global economy of the 21st century. Recent financial crises and trade tensions have only served to underline that the international system more than ever needs transparent and binding rules-based liberalisation as a pillar of development and a bulwark against protectionist pressures.

REAPING THE FULL BENEFITS OF OPEN MARKETS

I. INTRODUCTION

Liberalisation of trade and investment by non-OECD economies has been a dominant trend in the global economy in recent decades. Both developing and transition economies have been striving to accelerate their development by benefiting from the dynamism and the new opportunities in the global market place. However, concerns have been expressed that countries suffering from financial crises might turn away from open trade and investment. And widening current account imbalances in the OECD area have raised the risk of protectionist pressures. Against this background, this report discusses the benefits and some of the challenges of trade and investment for development.

These issues have been on the international agenda for some time, with the OECD contributing in many ways, including through the *OECD Development Partnerships Strategy*.[1] This is an integrated strategy based on helping developing countries build their own capacities for development, integration into the global economy, external assistance and improved "developmental coherence" in OECD Member countries' policies.

In a similar vein, President James Wolfensohn of the World Bank has launched a proposal to co-ordinate development co-operation around a *Comprehensive Development Framework*.[2] Country-level frameworks would be owned and managed by the developing countries themselves, rather than by donors or international agencies. Policies to further open to trade and investment would be closely co-ordinated with efforts in the areas of physical infrastructure, social investment and the improvement of the quality of governance and institutions.

The international trade and investment agenda has come to the forefront again in the wake of the global financial crisis and looking ahead to the Third WTO Ministerial Meeting in Seattle and to the launching of a broad-based Round of trade negotiations. The importance of leadership by OECD countries is highlighted by the hesitations of many developing countries about a possible new Round.

In this context, this report addresses the following specific issues:

- Trends in trade and investment liberalisation (Section II).

- Benefits of trade and investment for development (Section III).

- Some experiences of Korea, Mexico, transition economies, ASEAN4 (Indonesia, Malaysia, the Philippines and Thailand), Chile and the least developed countries (LDCs)[3] (Section IV).

- Policy challenges for benefiting from open trade and investment (Section V).

- Trade, investment, development, and the environment (Section VI).

- How international co-operation, including through the OECD, can strengthen the foundations for rapid and sustainable economic development (Section VII).

The conclusion of this report is that open trade and investment have indeed been a powerful tool for stimulating rapid and sustainable economic development. At the same time, it seems clear that open trade and investment are not alone sufficient, and give rise to many other policy challenges. Openness must be accompanied by a coherent set of growth-oriented macroeconomic and structural policies, capacity-building, adequate social policy and good governance in order to capture its full benefits for rapid and sustainable economic development. Further, countries like Korea and Mexico have demonstrated the positive developments that can result from liberalisation and structural reform as a response to economic crisis.

All countries have a coincidence of interests in pushing ahead with more open trade and investment. They also have a coincidence of interests in building strong policies and institutions for a well-functioning market economy. Each country's economic strength depends on the strength of its trading partners. Recent financial crises have highlighted the close and growing interdependence amongst the world's economies. All countries are working together through the whole range of international organisations, including the OECD, to secure sustainable development and integrate successfully into the global economy.

II.   TRENDS IN LIBERALISATION

(i)   OECD countries

Liberalisation of trade and investment has been a driving force in the rapid economic development of OECD countries in the post-war period. Eight rounds of multilateral trade negotiations have succeeded in lowering the average (trade-weighted) most-favoured-nation (MFN) tariff rates on industrial goods from a high of 40 per cent at the end of World War II to around 5 per cent at the end of the Uruguay Round. However, tariff reductions have not been even for all products and across main sectors.

While much progress has been achieved in lowering protection on industrial goods, considerable barriers to trade in agriculture remain in most OECD countries. Measures on the frequency of use of non-tariff barriers have declined, although many remain, including some regulatory measures that can act as barriers to trade.[4]

Policies in such areas as investment and competition can effectively buttress and thereby secure real access to markets. In nearly all OECD countries, restrictions on outward and inward foreign direct investment (FDI) in manufacturing have been substantially reduced over the past decade (the main investment focus of this report is FDI, which can be defined as ownership of assets in one country by residents of another for purposes of controlling the use of those assets). This has favoured increased FDI flows and contributed to the globalisation of production systems. However, a number of barriers remain in the service sector in most countries.

(ii)   Non-OECD economies

Liberalisation of trade and investment by non-OECD economies has been a dominant trend in the global economy in recent decades.[5] From the 1960s and 1970s, as four dynamic Asian economies (Hong Kong, China; Korea; Singapore; and Chinese Taipei) expanded their manufactured exports rapidly, the world trade and investment scene began changing markedly. Following in their footsteps, many other developing and then transition economies started abandoning state-led, inward-oriented strategies adopted in the post-War period, and are now active participants in world trade and investment.

Developing countries' share of world trade has now risen to 30 per cent, compared with less than 20 per cent fifteen years ago. And, particularly in the 1990s, they have seen a steady increase in FDI and large amounts of other more liquid private capital flows, like portfolio investment and bank credit. At the same time, the pace of integration of developing economies into the global economy has been very uneven. For example, Africa's share of world trade has continuously declined since the late 1960s, and the continent has been largely bypassed by the surge in private capital flows and is still overwhelmingly dependent on ODA.

International co-operation between all countries has been strengthening, in particular through multilateral trade liberalisation and the strengthening of the multilateral system, culminating with the Uruguay Round and the creation of WTO. Today, the WTO has 134 members, of which 80 per cent are developing or transition economies. And over 20 developing or transition economies are now negotiating to join.[6]

But, to what extent are non-OECD markets open? Even Hong Kong, China, the quintessential model of a free market, retains some restrictions on trade and investment. Overall, while most developing countries are now liberalising their trade and investment policies, many restrictions also remain.

On average, trade and investment restrictions in developing and transition countries (even the fast-growing ones) are higher than for developed countries. For example, after the Uruguay Round reductions, tariffs on imports from OECD countries average close to 11 per cent in developing countries and 8 per cent in transition economies, while OECD tariffs on imports from these two groups are around 5 and 4 per cent respectively.[7] The scale of restrictions on FDI and other capital flows is also much higher in non-OECD countries. Many developing and transition countries screen incoming investment, and retain extensive controls on foreign participation in particular sectors.

(iii)   The last two years

Current account imbalances in the OECD area have widened over the past two years, and raised concerns about related increases in protectionist sentiments. And in the wake of the financial crises in East Asia, Russia and then Brazil, concerns have also been expressed about the commitment to open trade and investment in crisis-affected countries. But, there has not been a general rise in protectionism. On the contrary. OECD countries are committed to resisting protectionist pressures. For their part, most crisis-affected countries are continuing to liberalise trade and investment, and strengthening domestic institutions and policies. They see liberalisation as the solution to the crisis, not the cause of it.

According to IMF estimates[8], during 1998 24 countries out of the total 173 IMF members for which data are available, increased their overall trade openness, while only 3 countries were estimated to have increased their overall degree of trade restrictiveness. These changes resulted in an overall increase from 79 to 87 in the number of countries whose trade systems could be classified as "open", while there has been a decline from 38 to 33 in the number of countries that could be classified as "restrictive" (the remaining countries are classified as "moderate").

(iv)   *Towards a new Round*

Trade and investment is being liberalised in several ways – autonomously, in regional integration arrangements and in the context of multilateral negotiations. Since the mid-1980s, over 60 developing countries have autonomously lowered their trade barriers. This enables them to capture immediate benefits from liberalisation and integrate trade liberalisation into coherent economic reform strategies.

Multilateral liberalisation can provide additional benefits. Domestic public support for liberalisation measures can be easier to secure when liberalisation is part of a global effort. And the benefits are greater when a country's liberalisation is accompanied by liberalisation from others. Measures taken within the framework of transparent and binding rules-based liberalisation also provide insurance against protectionist pressures, and can add credibility to individual countries' liberalisation process.

The next WTO Ministerial Conference, to be held in late 1999, will consider whether to launch a new Round of multilateral trade negotiations. OECD countries support a new Round of trade negotiations to further relax impediments to the movements of goods and services across countries, and as a stimulus to global economic activity.

While developing countries generally support trade and investment liberalisation, some still have reservations about a new Round, which they fear will be dominated by the interests of developed countries. Some are concerned that a new Round might divert attention from the scheduled implementation of commitments agreed during the Uruguay Round. These include the expected elimination by 2005 of quotas on imports of textiles and clothing, the implementation of guidelines in the areas of trade-related investment measures (TRIMs), trade-related aspects of intellectual property rights (TRIPs) and agriculture. Furthermore, under the Uruguay Round a range of selective negotiations, in the areas of trade in agriculture, trade in services and aspects of intellectual property, was already scheduled.

It is worth noting that similar reservations were also expressed prior to the launch of the Uruguay Round. In the event, developing countries participated actively in the Round and achieved some considerable success. For example, the participation of some major developing countries in the Cairns Group played a critical role in getting agriculture on the agenda. Developing countries also managed to negotiate the phasing out of the Multi-fibre Agreement, which was one of the most costly trade restrictions against their exports. In the end, developing countries gained much more out of the Uruguay Round than they had anticipated.[9]

A new Round of multilateral trade negotiations has the potential to offer great benefits to all countries. OECD countries need to show leadership in ensuring that the interests of all countries – developed, developing and transition economies – are taken into account. In this regard, OECD countries have a responsibility to consider the effect of their own policies on developing and transition economies, especially regarding market access. It is also important to support capacity-building in developing countries, and to accord particular priority to supporting growth in LDCs. The objectives for a Round should be to achieve substantial liberalisation, to further strengthen and consolidate the institutional and legal framework of the WTO, to keep its agenda relevant to rapid changes in the world economy, to advance thereby sustainable development and to ensure a fair and more open multilateral system that works for the benefit and welfare of all its Members and their peoples.

III.   BENEFITS OF OPEN TRADE AND INVESTMENT FOR ECONOMIC DEVELOPMENT

Economies with open trade and investment can: (i) specialise in what they are best at; (ii) create competitive industries; (iii) stimulate domestic and foreign investment; (iv) exploit economies of scale; and (v) benefit from transfers of knowledge, technology and organisational capacities, through access to new products and processes.

Careful interpretation should be made of the empirical evidence of the relationship between external openness and economic development. As always, there are exceptions to the observable pattern. However, empirical evidence confirms that the record of growth and poverty reduction achieved by developing countries which have liberalised trade and investment stands as one of the more remarkable episodes in the history of economic development. Open trade and investment have been beneficial for development, when accompanied by a coherent set of growth-oriented macroeconomic and structural policies, capacity-building, adequate social policy and good governance.

- Open economies have grown significantly faster than closed economies over sustained periods of time. Indeed, there are no recent examples of countries achieving sustained high rates of economic growth on the basis of "closed" economies. Almost all studies show trade policy to be a significant explanatory factor in growth, in association with sound macroeconomic and structural policies. For example, a study covering 89 developing economies found that per capita income growth of 15 "open economies" averaged some 4½ per cent over the period 1970 to 1989, compared with 0.7 per cent for economies that were not always open over this period.[10]

- Income levels of "open" developing economies have been converging towards those of OECD countries, as the former have achieved substantially higher per capita income growth than the OECD average (2.3 per cent from 1970-89). On the other hand, income levels of closed economies have fallen even further behind and income gaps have widened not just *vis-à-vis* "open" developing countries, but also the OECD average.

- The benefits of open trade and investment for economic development do not depend on initial income levels. Open economies at all levels of development have successfully increased their participation in world trade. The failure of many developing countries to generate convergent growth is policy-determined rather than due to low initial levels of development.[11]

- With open trade and investment generating higher growth, the evidence is that this growth has also been associated with reductions in poverty. For example, in a range of developing countries, 77 out of 88 decade-long periods of growth were accompanied by reductions in poverty. Indeed, on average the income of the poor tends to grow proportionately to the average income of the entire population, although there are cases where the income of the poor grows more slowly and more quickly than the average. In countries where incomes are initially fairly unequal, higher openness and growth work to reduce these inequalities, whereas in countries where incomes are initially fairly equal, higher openness and growth tend to make income shares less equal.[12]

- As open trade and investment has contributed to economic development, there has also been a positive association over time between successfully sustained trade reforms and improvements in core labour standards.[13]

IV.   SOME COUNTRY EXPERIENCES

While the general conclusions are clear, the experiences of developing and transition economies with open trade and investment are quite diverse. No country has perfectly open trade and investment regimes. Specific interventions have often been used: some with apparent success, and some with dramatic failure. And relative openness has generally been achieved progressively. The evidence suggests that to reap the full benefits of open trade and investment, it must be part of a coherent set of policies and reforms. And positive developments can result from liberalisation and structural reform as a response to economic crisis. This section presents some experiences of Korea, Mexico, some transition economies, the ASEAN4 (Indonesia, Malaysia, the Philippines and Thailand), Chile and the LDCs.

(i)   Korea

Korea's rapid export-oriented economic development was accompanied by extensive government intervention in the form of export promotion, import restrictions, subsidies and credit allocation.[14] Trade played a powerful role in Korea's development, through specialisation of production, economies of scale, the establishment of new industries and acquisition of new technology. Exporters relied on foreign buyers for product-design technology and for product improvement. This was particularly important since FDI, a common source of technology transfer, was greatly restricted in Korea.

This development record gave rise to two schools of thought – commonly labelled as neo-classical and revisionist. The neo-classical interpretation stresses the importance of getting the economic fundamentals right and attributes Korea's outstanding performance to its high level of investment, its sound fiscal policies, its heavy investment in education and its relative degree of openness to world markets. The revisionist interpretation, in contrast, argues that the government was able to improve the market outcome and accelerate economic growth by deliberately distorting prices and incentives.

The pattern of Korean growth over the past 35 years suggests that government interventions to distort prices and incentives were not a key factor in accelerating growth. Despite government policies to promote heavy and chemical industries, some of these industries had difficulty in becoming internationally competitive, and contributed to some of the vulnerabilities that led to the recent financial crisis. Other industries, such as electronics, have developed successfully with much less government guidance. Moreover, it is difficult to see major changes in Korea's economic performance over a long period with markedly different industry policies, but fairly stable economic fundamentals. A common factor in each phase of industrial policy, which limited the harmful effects of distorted prices and incentives, was the emphasis placed on exports as a criteria for firms that received credit and other forms of government assistance. Also, Korea had many other strengths, notably in the area of education and high savings and investment.

In the early 1980s, when worldwide recession and inflation struck, Korea's macroeconomic stabilisation programme was accompanied by liberalisation of structural policies, including substantial import liberalisation. The government was concerned about the adverse effects of extensive interventions on economic efficiency, particularly problems of over-investment in certain favoured sectors, which emerged in the wake of the heavy and chemical industries drive. Contrary to initial intentions, measures to liberalise financial markets and capital flows were much more limited. Reform efforts suffered from resistance by domestic vested interests and lack of political will to implement reforms.

Korea then returned to rapid economic development. While exports continued to play a leading role, in conjunction with Korea's underlying economic strengths, the government retained a dirigiste approach. As was ultimately evident in the recent financial crisis, this led to a dichotomy between on the one hand, strong economic growth, and on the other, weak profitability, an excessively indebted corporate sector and a poorly –supervised, shaky financial sector. These weaknesses stemmed from the fact that banks and corporations were linked closely with the government in a web of implicit guarantees that led to excessive risk-taking, over-investment and insufficient attention to credit and exchange rate risks. In addition, weak corporate governance practices led firms to emphasise size rather than creating shareholder value. Overall, this led to excess capacities in heavy industry, many bad loans and consequent banking sector difficulties.

The government-led development strategy, which had success in the 1970s and 1980s, proved ill-suited for an environment of global competition in the 1990s. The new Korean President capitalised on the financial crisis to rally public support for economic reform. Korea has made an impressive start in laying the groundwork for a more market-based paradigm, by exposing the economy more fully to competitive forces and introducing more effective governance structures into financial institutions and the corporate sector. Its dramatic reform measures include radically opening its capital account, racing well ahead of its accession-obligations under the OECD codes.

Korea is already rebounding from the crisis. The Korean won, which was essentially stable in the second half of 1998, has been on an upward trend in the first part of 1999, foreign capital has begun to flow back in very rapidly, including FDI, and stock prices have doubled since November 1998. GDP, which fell by almost 6 per cent in 1998, could grow by 6 ½ per cent in 1999. As in the early 1980s, Korea is again adjusting successfully to economic crisis thanks to liberalisation and structural reform. If sustained and deepened, these reforms would allow Korea to return to a high growth path by fully exploiting the benefits of open trade and investment.

(ii)   Mexico

Mexico has undergone an economic transformation in the last decade and a half that is extraordinary by any standards.[15] Before 1982, Mexico relied heavily on import-substitution policies, emphasising industrialisation and infrastructure development. Fledgling industries were shielded from import competition, and the costs of this protection were born by established economic activities.

Trade and foreign investment were carefully managed to protect infant industries. The overvaluation of the exchange rate allowed relatively cheap imports of essential industrial inputs, while less essential imports were physically rationed or excluded altogether. While these policies contributed to the establishment of an industrial base and the modernisation of the Mexican economy, their long-term success would inevitably be compromised by the limited size of the domestic market, and by inefficiency and a lack of competitiveness in several branches of economic activity. As most new industries concentrated on supplying the domestic market, exports played a limited role in economic growth, and were highly concentrated in the oil sector. By the time of the 1982 debt crisis, growth was already being hampered by the intrinsic limitations of the previous policies.

The trigger for an open trade and investment strategy, and other structural reforms was the problems of the 1980s, as the debt crisis was followed by five years of economic stagnation. Negotiation of an incomes policy stabilisation programme facilitated inflation reduction, which was also favoured by decisive trade and investment liberalisation and privatisation. Most state-owned enterprises were privatised, and new opportunities were opened for national and foreign investment in infrastructure. A modern competition law adopted in 1993 created an over-arching framework for market-based principles. Domestic reforms were underpinned by international commitments as Mexico joined the GATT, APEC and the OECD, and signed NAFTA and other free trade agreements.

21

To a great extent the liberalisation strategy worked. The economy returned to growth, with exports of manufactures playing an important role. Inflation fell continuously, large fiscal deficits were eliminated and the stock of government debt was reduced to one of the lowest levels in the OECD. Renewed confidence on the part of investors led to a rapid rise in capital flows, including FDI.

However, the Achilles heel remained the external accounts. Despite debt reduction efforts, the still outstanding debt required retaining confidence of foreign and domestic investors. And Mexico's inflation rate, while declining, remained above that of its trading partners, resulting in an underlying trend of real exchange rate appreciation. This trend was exacerbated by rapid growth in consumption and investment, thanks to the expansion of credit following financial sector reforms and large capital flows.

The result was a growing current account deficit -- from an average of 3 per cent of GDP in 1989-90 to 8 per cent in 1994 -- as exports began to slow and imports accelerated. The peso then came under increasing pressure, as capital outflows began to occur in mid-1994 at a time of internal political shocks and high US interest rates. Ultimately, the government was forced to devalue and then float the peso in December 1994, and Mexico entered its second major financial crisis in as many decades. The immediate consequences were devastating. The peso fell by 76 per cent against the dollar between December 1994 and May 1995, the stock market crashed by 40 per cent. And in 1995, GDP fell by 6.2 per cent, while real wages, consumption and investment fell even more, and almost 800,000 jobs were lost in the formal sector.

The financial crisis presented the danger of protectionist measures. But, instead of halting reforms, the new crisis reaffirmed Mexico's strong political willingness to continue reforming. Mexico signed free trade agreements with several Latin American countries, and opened several sectors previously closed to foreign investment (such as telecommunications and railroads). Mexico's trade and investment policies also benefited from international commitments such as the WTO and NAFTA. Structural change was accelerated by renovation in the political and public governance landscape, and by a government-wide deregulation programme that has been whittling away the myriad of forms in which the government intervened in economic activity. In the five years since Mexico signed the NAFTA in 1993, FDI averaged $10.5 billion/year, whereas in the five years before the agreement, FDI averaged less than $5 billion/year.

The Mexican government's stabilisation programme, buttressed by a package of international liquidity support, was a key factor in economic recovery. The Mexican economy rebounded quickly and strongly from the crisis of 1994/95.

GDP growth averaged 5.6 per cent from 1996 to 1998. Close to 2 million jobs were created from late 1995 through 1997, with exports accounting for most of the jobs created since 1995.

A number of features differentiate the recovery since 1995 from the one following the 1982 debt crisis. In the current cycle, exports have not been the only engine of growth. Investment, particularly in export-oriented firms, has also expanded at very rapid rates, followed more recently by private consumption. Moreover, the longevity of the export boom has been different. While in the initial stages of both cycles Mexican producers were able to re-orient their activities towards the export sector, in 1982-85 the export boom fizzled out as soon as domestic demand started to recover. This was due to the fact that productive capacity had not been increased sufficiently and the manufacturing export base was narrow. In the current upswing, on the other hand, high levels of capacity created by several years of buoyant investment in export-oriented firms have allowed the rapid expansion of exports to continue even as domestic demand picked up. Finally, while high import tariffs and quotas were used to face the 1982 crisis, imports were not restricted on this occasion, so as to favour access to inputs and facilitate recovery.

The international financial crisis and the fall in oil prices in 1998 caused the peso to depreciate and required successive tightenings of macroeconomic policies to preserve confidence and curb the deterioration of the external balance. While output growth is expected to slow down in 1999, with a progressive return of confidence in international financial markets, it is expected to strengthen again in 2000. Compared with the situation in 1994, the exchange rate is now floating and the authorities are committed to taking action to stabilise the economy. The last year has shown that it is now possible to deal with external shocks in a more timely and, hence, effective way than in the past. Further, Mexico's solid economic fundamentals have enabled international investors to differentiate it from other countries in the context of the recent financial instability.

The experience of Mexico indicates the positive developments that can result from stabilisation, liberalisation and structural reforms as a response to economic crisis. However, to strengthen further the resilience of the Mexican economy to shocks and improve the foundations for sustainable economic growth, an important policy agenda remains ahead, particularly in the areas of physical infrastructure and human capital development, where the social and economic returns are potentially high.

(iii)   Transition economies

Trade and investment liberalisation was an integral part of the 'first generation' of economic reforms implemented by transition economies after the fall of the communist system.[16] The opening of their economies to the outside world was considered critical to overcome the legacies of central planning, notably a distorted and administered price system, lagging productivity and technological backwardness.

Such liberalisation must however occur concurrently with wide-ranging structural transformation in order to sustain and build on progress as it occurs. Privatisation and competition policy are key, as they facilitate the entry of new firms and discourage market concentration that might allow protectionist alliances among major producers to emerge.   Labour market policies also support liberalisation by encouraging the mobility of the workforce, especially from inefficient to internationally-competitive sectors and firms. Structural improvements in the banking system (and capital markets more generally, in light of the prospective important of portfolio flows) also facilitate liberalisation, since poorly functioning banks reduce the efficiency of foreign-trade operations and make the financing of modernisation requirements difficult and expensive. A solid legal foundation, with clear and predictable regulations, is another prerequisite, as legal uncertainty and the inadequate enforcement of contracts discourage firms from investing and modernising their production facilities.

The extent of trade and investment reform has varied from country to country, reflecting differences in initial economic conditions and the approach taken to reform.   The central and eastern European countries (CEECs) had fewer impediments than the other ex-communist territories, more rapid and successful macroeconomic stabilisation and geographical proximity to alternative markets, all of which facilitated rapid progress in trade and investment liberalisation.

Dynamic exports and large flows of FDI have been a strong growth factor for those CEECs that have undertaken substantial and wide-ranging structural reforms. Over the last five years, exports have grown particularly strongly for Hungary (annual average growth rate of 21 per cent), Poland (13 per cent) and the Czech Republic (10 per cent). And following the contractions in foreign trade that resulted from the collapse of the Council for Mutual Economic Assistance (CMEA), exports have also been successfully redirected to western markets, which are now the destination for two-thirds or more of exports. These same economies have also managed to attract large amounts of FDI over the period 1990 to 1998 (Poland -- $23 billion, Hungary - $17 billion and Czech

Republic -- $7 billion), which has played an important role in enhancing economic efficiency.

Trade and investment liberalisation has faced more serious obstacles in the New Independent States of the ex-Soviet Union (NIS). While most CEECs had been liberalising, to some degree, policies for trade with the West since the 1960s, the Soviet Union remained essentially a closed economy. The Soviet Union also possessed a structure of manufacturing that was relatively less favourable for international competitiveness, including a high concentration in the defence industry. Its dependency on cheap energy was also a very important factor, and partly explains why the economic contraction was so severe following liberalisation in 1992. Further, attitudes and legislation in the area of FDI have been more problematic in much of the NIS relative to the CEECs.

The NIS, with the exception of Russia, were less familiar with applying basic trade instruments and inexperienced with the laws and institutions of trade and investment policies. Moreover, their uneven progress in macro-economic stabilisation, high inflation rates and volatile exchange rates have continued to blur price signals, thus preventing domestic producers from adopting longer-term strategies. Delays in structural reforms - privatisation and competition policy in particular - have also hampered trade and investment liberalisation, since powerful sector-specific lobbies with privileged links to governments (in the automobile sector, for instance) often resist liberalisation efforts.

Support by OECD countries has been very important for trade reform in the NIS and CEECs. In 1990-93, these countries were granted most-favoured nation (MFN) status and general system of preferences (GSP) benefits, and most quantitative restrictions that targeted former socialist countries were eliminated. Preferential trade agreements have improved market access, especially after the signature of the comprehensive and far-reaching Europe Agreements concluded between ten CEECs (including the Baltic states) and the European Union. Nevertheless, a range of restrictive measures continues to hamper exporters in the CEECs and NIS. These restrictions are often concentrated in so-called 'sensitive sectors', such as agricultural products, steel, footwear, textiles and clothing. These are still subject to relatively high tariff and non-tariff barriers, while some transition countries would appear to have considerable export potential in these areas.

Recent economic and trade performance of individual transition countries, in particular their resistance to contagion effects of the financial crises in Russia, East Asia and Brazil, has benefited from their macroeconomic stabilisation efforts, and structural reforms which have strengthened their resilience to shocks, as well as their success in reorienting and diversifying their exports and attracting durable investment flows. For instance, both Hungary and Poland weathered the financial market turmoil surrounding the Russian crisis with limited permanent impact, and in 1998 achieved growth rates among the highest in the OECD area, notwithstanding some slowdown in export growth.[17]

(iv)   ASEAN4

FDI has played an important role in the economic development of Indonesia, Malaysia, the Philippines and Thailand (ASEAN4), particularly in export sectors like electronics and automobiles, and has been an important stable source of capital during the recent financial crisis.[18]   It has helped transform these economies from exporters of agricultural products and raw materials, into major producers and exporters of manufactured goods. The ASEAN4 have collectively become among the most important destinations for FDI outside of the OECD area.

FDI, like other capital flows, facilitates investment beyond what could be achieved by domestic savings alone. In addition, FDI can enhance the level of competition in an economy and bring in ideas, innovations, expertise and other forms of technology. Multinational enterprises, with their global network of affiliates, can also channel exports from the host country to affiliates elsewhere in the form of intra-firm trade. Nevertheless, experience with FDI shows that these benefits are not necessarily automatic.

The ASEAN4 have, to varying degrees, welcomed inward investment for its contribution to exports. Indeed, aggressive attempts have been made to promote export-oriented investments, particularly those locating in export processing zones, which are given numerous incentives in all four countries, including automatic approvals, land ownership, the possibility of full control of the affiliate, tax holidays and duty free imports of components.

But, this has led to a dualist policy towards inward investment. In spite of openness to export-oriented projects, these countries still maintain numerous restrictions on inward investment for domestic market-oriented projects. All four countries routinely screen inward investment; some sectors are proscribed for foreign investors; equity limits often apply in other sectors and for acquisitions of local companies; and land ownership is sometimes restricted.

These restrictions have served to protect inefficient local producers, to limit the local content of exports and to impede potential technology transfers. The ASEAN4 have not always managed to translate economic growth through FDI into something more durable which builds on existing indigenous capabilities.

26

An important mechanism for technology transfer is through the linkages between firms, as local firms co-operate with foreign investors either as joint venture partners or as suppliers. Government efforts to enhance these linkages have not often been successful. Another reason for the poor performance in technology transfer is that the capacity of local workers and management to employ foreign technologies is weak. In sum, selective openness and policy deficiencies in other areas mean that the benefits of open trade and investment can not be fully captured.

A number of reform measures have been undertaken as a result of the crisis. Nevertheless, it is perhaps surprising (given the urgent need to bring in capital and to recapitalise local firms) how difficult it has been to pass legislation through parliaments -- local business interests sometimes represent a powerful lobby against any changes. Further, there is a risk that policymakers' preoccupation with crisis management will divert attention away from developing human resource and infrastructure capacities.

(v)   Chile

Perhaps no other country better reflects the rapid and difficult political and economic transformations that have occurred in Latin America over the last two decades or so.[19] Until the early 1970s, Chile had pursued an import substitution strategy for four decades, which resulted in increasingly poor economic performance and growing macroeconomic imbalances. It then went through two periods of deep structural reforms (including trade and investment) and macroeconomic stabilisation efforts (1975-80 and 1986 to date) separated by a period of financial crisis (1980-82) during which some reforms were reversed and priority was given to stabilisation policies.

In 1974/75, the Chilean government launched a very impressive trade and investment liberalisation programme. It also undertook a large number of other reform measures, including privatisation, deregulation, abolishing the multiple exchange rate regime and fiscal tightening. In 1979, the government began pegging the nominal exchange rate to the US dollar, as an anchor against inflation. However, since domestic inflation remained higher than international inflation, the exchange rate gradually appreciated in real terms. The gradual overvaluation of the currency stifled the export sector, and slowed down adjustment in the import competing sector, and the current account reached record high levels.

Pegging the exchange rate to an international currency can help restore confidence in the currency and encourage capital repatriation. But it must be backed by appropriate macroeconomic and structural policies. Otherwise, the real exchange rate can appreciate and undermine the objectives of trade and investment liberalisation, and other structural reforms. The large current account deficit was financed by foreign borrowing, and Chile like many other Latin American countries found itself in a debt crisis in 1982.

Management of the crisis involved strong stabilisation policies, and in the initial stages some trade policy reversals in an effort to reduce the large balance of payments deficit. The uniform tariff rate increased from 10 per cent to 20 per cent in 1983, and then to 35 per cent in 1984 as a means of generating higher government revenues and sharply reducing imports.

In 1985, Chile resumed an adjustment programme focused on export-oriented growth. Import barriers were then progressively reduced, many regulatory reforms undertaken, FDI laws liberalised, capital markets liberalised, bank supervision strengthened, and privatisation renewed. To complement the structural adjustment and trade reform measures, the macroeconomic policy mix aimed at achieving a competitive real exchange rate, and stable fiscal and monetary policies.

Chile's economic performance over the last decade has been remarkably strong, thanks to a combination of prudent fiscal and monetary policies, stringent financial sector supervision, important structural reforms, trade and investment liberalisation, and efforts to improve social conditions. However, reform policies during the 1990s have given priority to macroeconomic stability; structural reform initiatives have been less intense than in the 1980s. The gradual approach to the opening of the capital account and the introduction of restrictions to short-term capital inflows in 1991 (the URR or encaje, now in suspension) provide an illustration. Governments of the 1990s have also focused on human resource development as a means of supporting long term, sustainable growth.

Between 1989 and 1997, GDP doubled in real terms (although Chile has been in recession over the last six months), with strong exports (both copper and non-copper) and FDI playing important roles. In 1998, FDI inflows were $6 billion (about 9 per cent of GDP). Chile has now experienced five consecutive years of single-digit and continuously declining inflation. And the incidence of poverty has declined significantly, from nearly 40 per cent of the population in 1990 to 23 per cent in 1996.

Trade and investment liberalisation were ultimately successful, and have been a major factor in Chile's strong development over the last decade and a half. But this was made possible by improved coherence between trade and investment and other structural policies, and fiscal and exchange rate policies.

(vi) *Can the least developed countries benefit from open trade and investment ?*

The LDCs have not, as a group, been able to exploit the potential benefits of open trade and investment. Trade accounts for a very small percentage of GDP -- LDC exports represent around 9 percent of GDP versus 24 percent for all developing countries, while LDC imports are around 16 percent of GDP versus 26 percent for all developing countries. Moreover, LDCs' share in global exports fell from 0.8 in 1980 to 0.4 percent in 1997.[20] A similar story can be told for capital flows. The LDCs have grown more dependent on official development assistance to finance a growing share of their investment. And average per capita incomes in the LDCs have stagnated over the last two decades.

Over the last decade, the LDCs have been liberalising their trade and investment policies -- although, according to the IMF estimates, their trade policies remain more restrictive than the rest of the world.[21] And real GDP growth improved markedly during 1995-98, compared with the first half of the decade. However, developments over the last two years have adversely affected growth prospects for the LDCs, as demand and prices of their exports have fallen, and external financing conditions tightened.

Several factors have been suggested to explain the disappointing longer term performance of the LDCs: (a) high concentration of exports in commodities with a declining share in world trade and weak prices; (b) the structure of trade barriers facing LDC exports; and (c) weak domestic supply capacities. In fact, while LDC exports are highly concentrated on commodities -- just 20 products account for almost 70 percent of total exports -- LDCs have also suffered significant losses of market shares for their exports. Significant trade barriers exist in areas where the LDCs have a potential comparative advantage, notably agriculture and textiles. At the same time, trade preferences can give LDC exporters an edge over a large number of competitors.

The benefits from trade and investment liberalisation, and access to foreign markets do not come automatically, and require strong domestic policy frameworks. Most of the LDCs, face very difficult conditions, such as low human capital, poor resource bases, and political instability - including civil wars and regional conflicts. And high growth rates of population have undermined efforts to increase the average levels of education and health.

These factors have inhibited growth prospects, as have their high levels of debt, macroeconomic instability, poor governance and commodity price shocks.

Thus, in addition to liberalising their trade and investment policies, the LDCs need to reform many areas of public policy, especially to achieve universal access to basic social services, notably quality basic education and health care, reproductive health, sanitation and safe drinking water. Infrastructure is a particularly crucial issue for participation in the global economy, especially commercial and transport infrastructure capable of linking with global markets. But export competitiveness is often severely undermined by high transport costs in highly regulated shipping and airline industries. State of the art computer links are now indispensable even for very poor countries. Fortunately there are many new ways of approaching infrastructure provision and financing which developing countries can and are adopting to meet the large demanding requirements of the future.

What is the role of external assistance in facilitating the development of the LDCs?

- The emergence of an entrepreneurial economy transforms financing patterns from aid dependence to reliance on growing domestic savings, supplemented by international financial markets and foreign direct investment. But this takes time. In the meantime, official development assistance provides key support for social investment and the strengthening of participatory development and good governance. This highlights the importance of substantial levels of official development assistance, in particular for the poorest countries, as a means of helping developing countries maximise their prospects for growth.

- Development co-operation is also focusing on capacity-building, from infrastructure and institutions, to health care, education and social policy. To strengthen capacity development, the October 1997 WTO High Level Meeting established an Integrated Framework for Least Developed Countries Trade Development. This provides for the first time a systematic approach to helping LDCs to assess their needs and to co-ordinate technical assistance in three areas: the management of trade policy; export supply capabilities; and trade support services.

- The international community has been implementing debt relief through the Initiative for Heavily Indebted Poor

Countries (HIPC). This will only be effective if it complements and reinforces the reform efforts of debtor countries and lead to an increase in resource flows. It is necessary, however, to re-establish the creditworthiness of highly indebted countries, in order to underpin private sector-led development, as well as to create the fiscal space for higher social investment. This underscores the importance of the recent G8 initiative to further strengthen the HIPC Initiative.

- Some LDCs claim that they gained little out of the Uruguay Round, have difficulties implementing Uruguay Round commitments and have hesitations about a possible new Round of trade negotiations. However, a new Round would also represent a unique opportunity for addressing the concerns of LDCs and facilitating their integration into the multilateral system.

****

The above cases show that the impact of individual policies will always remain a subject of discussion, and that fundamentally the overall mix of policies is important. Further, within a basket of policies, some may be inefficient, and the key to sustained progress is that governments adapt and adjust these all along the way. Korea and Mexico provide examples of the positive developments that can result from liberalisation and structural reform as a response to economic crisis. For their part, both Hungary and Poland have weathered the financial turmoil surrounding the Russian crisis thanks to previous macroeconomic stabilisation efforts and success in reorienting and diversifying their exports and attracting durable investment flows.

Overall, open trade and investment must be part of a coherent and mutually reinforcing set of policies and reforms in order to capture its full benefits for rapid and sustainable economic development. However, the ASEAN4 have not been fully capturing the benefits of trade and investment due to selective openness and other policy deficiencies. Over the last decade and a half, Chile has reaped large benefits from trade and investment, thanks to improved coherence between trade and investment, and macro and structural policies. In the case of the LDCs, it will be necessary to strengthen greatly domestic policy frameworks to reap the full benefits of trade and investment. But external assistance also has an important role to play, notably through additional debt relief under appropriate conditions for deeply indebted developing countries.

V. WHAT OTHER POLICY CHALLENGES MUST BE TACKLED FOR BENEFITING FROM OPEN TRADE AND INVESTMENT?

It goes without saying that developing countries are at various stages of development. One-size policies won't fit all. The domestic policy challenges for realising the benefits of open trade and investment can differ greatly between developing countries.

Experience has shown that policy success is not necessary in all areas in order to benefit from open trade and investment, although a minimum threshold of good policies is required. Nevertheless, as evidenced by recent financial crises, policy deficiencies in certain areas can create serious fragilities and vulnerabilities.

This section reviews some of the key policy challenges for reaping fully the benefits of open trade and investment.

(i)   *Macroeconomic stability*

Stable and sustainable macroeconomic policy is a precondition for taking full advantage of the opportunities offered by globalisation, as well as for successful structural reform. Recent financial crises have highlighted the importance of avoiding large external imbalances and overvalued exchange rates. Low inflation rates and sustainable fiscal positions reduce the riskiness and improve the allocation of savings and investment, thereby stimulating economic development.

In East Asia, many governments have had great success in achieving low inflation and budget surpluses. This has been in sharp contrast to Latin America, where many countries were plagued by hyperinflation in the 1980s. Most Latin American countries have since made dramatic progress in stabilising, liberalising and restructuring their economies. But the process of stabilising fiscal and monetary imbalances has not always been easy, as the problems in Brazil testify. In many of the LDCs, macroeconomic stability remains elusive, with many countries suffering from high debt burdens.

(ii)   *Governance*

The key to the emergence of a vibrant market economy in a developing country (and historically in OECD countries) is the quality of governance and the level of trust among networks of economic actors. How successfully and how generally the market economy is able to spread in a country depends on the degree of peace and security, the existence of predictable, clean and accountable government, and the rule of law backed up by an effective legal system.

The main elements of better systems of governance are:

- An institutional and legal framework which supports the emergence of an enterprise-based economy and an efficient public sector.

- rising levels of participation in economic and political life as a basis for broadly-based growth, social cohesion and effective democratic institutions.

- The development of a competitive environment which enhances the efficient functioning of markets.

- A good corporate governance framework providing for transparency of corporate structures and operations and the accountability of management; and

- Vigorous action to fight corruption and organised crime.

There has been a general recognition within most countries that real economic benefits flow from improving the institutional and policy environment. But the speed and nature of the transition to better institutions is uneven. In East Asia, democracy has gained ground and governance issues generally are being addressed more openly. At the same time, there is still an important agenda of governance issues ahead for some countries in the region. The 1980s were a watershed for many Latin American countries. Democratically elected governments began to replace military dictatorships. In many of the developing countries at risk of being marginalised in the global economy, the requirements for good governance are seriously compromised or even effectively absent.

(iii)   *Financial and corporate sector strengthening*

The recent financial crisis has highlighted the importance of a number of policy requirements for strengthening financial and corporate sectors in developing countries (as well as the need for more sound behaviour by OECD private investors and creditors), namely:

- modernising and strengthening financial systems and upgrading regulatory and supervisory frameworks to encourage rigorous risk assessment and market discipline through increased disclosure and transparency; and ensuring that regulators and supervisors have the resources and support to do their job effectively; and

- reforming systems of corporate governance, competition policy and taxation, and countering bribery.

The liberalisation of financial services brings in the expertise of foreign institutions to help strengthen the capacity in developing countries to manage these flows and operate local financial markets effectively. It is also certain that well-functioning domestic financial markets are supported by macroeconomic stability, and flexible product and labour markets, which can help reduce the cost of adjustment of the real sector in the event of adverse financial shocks.

(iv)   *Human resource development*

Human resource development can have a significant positive impact on economic growth in open economies, but far less in closed economies.[22] This is an area where many East Asian governments have had great success. It has been estimated that high school enrolment rates in East Asia accounted for 38 per cent of the predicted difference in economic growth between East Asia and Latin America in 1960-90.[23] Many of the high growth economies in East Asia have had the combination of outward-oriented policies and high literacy rates. This was notably the case in Korea, whose literacy rate was already 71 per cent in 1960 compared with an average of 29 per cent in other low-income countries.[24] By contrast, Argentina, which pursued inward-looking policies, was unable to achieve sustainable economic growth until the last decade, despite its well-educated population.

However, even before the present financial crisis, strains were already showing in East Asia, especially in Thailand and Indonesia, with shortages in the supply of skilled labour. In Latin America, most countries suffer from persistent income disparities, and have a challenging agenda for human resource development. Among many of the poorer countries, high growth rates of population have undermined efforts to increase the average levels of education.

(v)   *Managing adjustment*

Successful economic development involves major structural adjustment, through a comprehensive process of societal change, with wide-ranging economic, social and political dimensions. Government policies stimulate these adjustment processes, when development is promoted through liberalisation of both trade and investment policies, and other reforms. In a rapidly growing economy, these policies can indeed facilitate the freeing of resources to other sectors and relieve resource bottlenecks. The experience of the emerging economies of East Asia shows rapid development and structural change can take place, while maintaining very low rates of unemployment.

Nevertheless, concerns are often expressed about the pace of trade and investment liberalisation, as much as the direction of policy change. Liberalisation is not always and everywhere painless, and can create hardship for some workers, firms, and the communities in which they are located. The key challenge is to spread the gains from expanded trade and investment more widely in the population and across countries through effective structural adjustment policies, and the development of new social frameworks and safety nets.

A system of social protection is a central ingredient of public action to help provide safeguards against adverse shocks, especially for those at risk of irreversible declines in their human, social or physical assets. It is important that formal social protection be designed in a fashion that does not give incentives for permanent dependency, and integrated into policies to get people into employment. However, in most developing countries, the bulk of the population falls outside formal systems of social protection. They rely primarily on family and community-based mechanisms for managing risk and caring for those excluded from economic progress.

Such informal mechanisms of risk management and protection are especially under stress in the context of local or economy-wide shocks. Hence, in addition to systems for the formal sector, it is critical to develop policies and institutions that extend access to basic services, and strengthen risk management for the vulnerable – and which do so in a fashion that is consistent with a country's level of development, designed to be sustainable, and supportive of informal mechanisms.

VI. TRADE, INVESTMENT AND DEVELOPMENT, AND THE ENVIRONMENT

Trade, investment, and rapid technological advances are changing the nature and the level of environmental stresses in both developing and developed countries.[25] In some circumstances, open trade and investment policies will contribute to improved environmental conditions. They do this by improving the efficiency of environmental resource use, by reducing existing distortions which may already be damaging the environment, and by promoting the development, transfer, and adoption of more environmentally-friendly technologies.

On the other hand, liberalisation will also amplify and/or redistribute environmental pressures in certain areas of economic activity. These "scale" and "structural" effects" are most likely to appear in economic sectors where high-volume/low-margin products closely related to the exploitation of the natural environment are involved (e.g. resource-using sectors).

The challenge will be to reduce the potential negative environmental effects of liberalisation, and to promote the positive ones. Developing countries may be particularly vulnerable to the environmental pressures associated with liberalisation, for two basic reasons. First, the local governance situation in developing countries may be relatively weak, implying that local environmental regulations will not always be set (or enforced) at levels which provide adequate environmental protection. Second, the relative weight of developing countries in generating global environmental pressures seems likely to grow in the future, as these economies develop. (The non-OECD share of world GDP could rise from about 40 per cent in 1995, to over 60 per cent in 2020[26].) If these shifts come to pass, the developing countries may come under increasing economic pressure from the developed countries to reduce the related environmental stresses on the regional or global environments.

The empirical evidence of the environmental effects of open trade and investment policies is mixed. There have been cases reported of environmental harm associated with liberalised investment or trade flows (again, most notably in the natural resource-using sectors). Against that, there is also evidence that foreign firms or products commonly embody better environmental practices and technologies. For example, foreign firms are often the first to respond to consumer pressures for "greener" products or production methods. On balance, available evidence is not yet conclusive about the net environmental effects of liberalisation.

The institutional and regulatory context in which the trade and investment takes place is clearly a critical determinant of these net environmental effects, and thus, of the sustainability of economic development. Establishing sound national policies and institutional frameworks for environmental management in developing countries is therefore necessary if the material gains from intensified trade and investment flows are to strengthen environmental progress.

However, many developing countries, and particularly the LDCs, still lack the basic capacity to establish and enforce appropriate laws and regulations. Important weaknesses include a lack of regulatory stability and transparency, as well as a shortage of expertise in areas such as negotiating, contracting and competitive bidding. In some economic sectors, this may make it more difficult to ensure the necessary balance of benefits between investors and host countries, and may eventually result in increased pollution and unsustainable production patterns. Unpredictable regulatory regimes also encourage short-term rent-seeking behaviour and act as a deterrent to long-term investment. Accordingly, development co-operation efforts are seeking to help developing countries establish the economic, legal and regulatory frameworks necessary to provide a stable and attractive investment climate, while ensuring compliance environmental rules and safeguards. In partial response to this problem, many developing countries formulated national strategies for sustainable development, in the wake of the Rio Conference in 1992.

There is also a strong need to improve the coherence of trade, investment, development and environment policies at national, regional, and international levels, so that they are complementary and mutually reinforcing. This need is reflected not only in debates about the inclusion of trade measures in certain multilateral environmental agreements, but also in discussions about the use of certain types of environmental measures (e.g. eco-labelling and packaging rules) that could act as non-tariff barriers to trade, by restricting market access. This latter issue is particularly important for developing countries. The demand for "green" products could result in more opportunities and market advantages for developing countries in sectors where their traditional products and production methods are "environmentally friendly". Against that, stringent and numerous environmental requirements, which do not take account of regional and local conditions, could serve to hinder trading opportunities in the developing world.

VII.   ROLE OF INTERNATIONAL CO-OPERATION

Today's globalising world economy generates a coincidence of interests for all countries -- in pushing ahead with more open trade and investment, and in building strong policies and institutions for a well-functioning market economy. Strong trade and investment partners are necessary to achieve increased prosperity, greater political security and environmental sustainability in the 21st century.

All countries – developed, developing and transition -- are working together through the whole range of international institutions, including the OECD, to secure sustainable development and integrate successfully into the global economy. In particular, they are seeking to strengthen policies and institutions, and to address systemic issues at both the national and global levels in order to build a robust global economy, in which flows of trade, investment and knowledge deliver mutual benefits.

The OECD has a wide range of activities for policy dialogue between Members and non-members, which enable non-members to participate in and contribute to the Organisation's work. The priority themes are issues of importance for the successful integration of non-member economies into the international economic system, notably in areas like trade, investment, corporate governance, regulatory reform, tax policy, competition, fiscal reform, anti-bribery, public sector governance, the environment and social policy.

OECD Member countries have an important leadership role to play, in light of their predominant share in world output, trade and capital flows. In this context, the OECD is working with its Member countries, based on its multi-disciplinary analysis and monitoring and surveillance activities to:

- Strengthen the framework for international trade flows by resisting protectionist pressures, maintaining open markets and sustaining the momentum of liberalisation;

- Strengthen also the framework for international investment and capital flows; and

- Survey progress made in the implementation of the OECD Development Partnerships Strategy – notably for the impact of OECD countries' policies on the sustainable development of developing economies.

A priority issue is the preparation for a broad-based new Round of multilateral negotiations. All countries have a vital stake in a new Round to prepare for the global economy of the 21st century. Recent tensions have only served to underline that the international system more than ever needs transparent and binding rules-based liberalisation as a pillar of development and a bulwark against protectionist pressures. A new Round would also provide an opportunity to integrate more fully the objective of sustainable development into the multilateral system, thereby ensuring more operationally effective and mutually reinforcing approaches to trade, environment, development and growth.

NOTES

1. DAC, OECD (1996).

2. World Bank (1999).

3. The term "Least Developed Countries", refers to the list of 48 countries classified by the UN as least developed and comprises Afganistan, Angola, Bangladesh, Benin, Bhutan, Burkina Faso, Burundi, Cambodia, Cape Verde, Central African Republic, Chad, Comoros, Congo Democratic Republic, Djibouti, Equatorial Guinea, Eritrea, Ethiopia, Gambia, Guinea, Guinea Bissau, Haiti, Kiribata, Laos, Lesotho, Liberia, Madagascar, Malawi, Maldives, Mali, Mauritania, Mozambique, Myanmar, Nepal, Niger, Rwanda, Sao Tome and Principe, Sierra Leone, Solomon Islands, Somalia, Sudan, Tanzania, Togo, Tuvalu, Uganda, Vanuatu, Western Somoa, Yemen and Zambia. 29 of the 48 LDCs are members of the WTO, while another 9 have observer status.

4. OECD(1999a).

5. OECD (1997e).

6. WTO (1998a).

7. OECD (1997e).

8. IMF (1999a).

9. Srinivasan (1988) and Safadi and Laird (1996).

10. Sachs, Jeffrey and Andrew Warner (1995). "Openness" was broadly defined to mean a decisive shift away from state-led industrialisation with high levels of protection which was the dominant development model adopted after World War II. An economy was classified as "closed" if it had any one of the following features: non-tariff barriers covering 40 per cent or more of trade; average tariff rates of 40 per cent or more; a black market exchange rate more than 20 per cent below the official rate; a socialist economic system; a state monopoly on major exports.

11 .   Low, Patrick, M. Olarraega and J. Suarez (1998).

12 .   Deininger, K. and L. Squire (1996).

13 .   OECD (1997), WTO (1998).

14 .   OECD, Economic Surveys of Korea, 1994, 1996, 1998.

15 .   OECD(1997b), OECD Economic Surveys of Mexico, 1996, 1998, 1999

16 .   Kalinova (1998).

17 .   OECD (1999a).

18 .   OECD (1999c).

19 .   OECD (1994a).

20 .   OECD (1997d).

21 .   IMF (1999b).

22 .   O'Connor and Lunati (1999)

23 .   World Bank (1993).

24 .   OECD Economic Survey of Korea, 1994.

25 .   OECD (1999d).

26.   OECD (1997e).

BIBLIOGRAPHY

SELECTED REFERENCES

OECD References

BERTHELEMY, J-C., S. Dessus and A. Varoudakis (1997), *Human Capital and Growth: The Role of the Trade Regime*, OECD Development Centre Studies.

DEVELOPMENT ASSISTANCE COMMITTEE (1996), *Shaping the 21st Century: The Contribution of Development Co-operation*, OECD.

DEVELOPMENT ASSISTANCE COMMITTEE (1997), (1998), *Efforts and Policies of the Members of the Development Assistance Committee*, OECD.

HIEMENZ, U. (1999), *Growth and Competition in the New Global Economy*, OECD Development Centre Seminar Series.

KALINOVA, B., "Trade Liberalisation in the Transition Economies", OECD Observer (1998), No.211: April/May.

MADDISON, A. (1989), *The World Economy in the 20th Century*, OECD Development Centre Studies.

MADDISON, A. (1995), *Monitoring the World Economy*, OECD Development Centre Studies.

O'CONNOR, D. and M.R.Lunati, Economic Opening and the Demand for Skills in Developing Countries: A Review of Theory and Evidence, OECD Development Centre, Technical Papers, No.149.

OECD *Economic Survey of Czech Republic*, 1998

OECD *Economic Survey of Hungary*, 1999

OECD *Economic Surveys of Korea,* 1994, 1996, 1998.

OECD *Economic Surveys of Mexico,* 1996, 1998, 1999

OECD *Economic Survey of Poland,* 1998

OECD (1994a), Benefits of Free Trade: East Asia and Latin America.

OECD (1994b), Report on Trade and Environment to the OECD Council at Ministerial Level.

OECD (1995a), "Emerging Markets and the Liberalisation of Capital Movements", in *OECD Economic Outlook*, No. 58.

OECD (1995b), *New Dimensions of Market Access in a Globalising World Economy.*

OECD (1996a), "Globalisation, Trade and Competition", *The OECD Observer* No. 201, August-September.

OECD (1996b), *Trade, Employment and Labor Standards: A Study of Core Workers' Rights and International Trade.*

OECD (1997a), *Economic Globalisation and the Environment.*

OECD (1997b), *Trade Liberalisation Policies in Mexico*

OECD (1997c), Globalisation and Linkages to 2020: Can Poor Countries and Poor People Prosper in the New Global Age?.

OECD (1997d), Market Access for the Least Developed Countries, Where Are the Obstacles?, Report submitted to the High Level Meeting on the Least Developed Countries in Geneva in 1997. [General Distribution, (OCDE/GD(97)174)].

OECD (1997e), *The World in 2020: Towards a New Global Age.*

OECD (1998a) Economic Outlook No. 64, December.

OECD (1998b), *Foreign Direct Investment and Economic Development: Lessons from Six Emerging Economies.*

OECD (1998c), "Foreign Direct Investment and the Environment: A Literature Review".

OECD (1998d), *Open Markets Matter: The Benefits of Trade and Investment Liberalisation.*

OECD (1999a) Economic Outlook No. 65, May.

OECD (1999b, forthcoming), *Foreign Direct Investment and Environment,* OECD Conference Proceedings.

OECD (1999c), *Foreign Direct Investment and Recovery in Southeast Asia,* OECD Conference Proceedings.

OECD (1999d), Interim Report of the OECD Three Year Project on Sustainable Development.

PORET, P. (1998), Liberalising Capital Flows: Lessons From Asia, OECD Observer, No.214: October/November.

REISEN, H. (1998), "After the Great Asian Slump: Towards a Coherent Approach to Global Capital Flows", Policy Brief No. 16, OECD Development Centre.

Other references

ASIAN DEVELOPMENT BANK INSTITUTE (1998), *Asia: Responding to Crisis.*

BLOMSTROM, M., R.E.Lipsey and Z. Zejan (August 1992), "What Explains Developing Country Growth?", NBER Working Paper No. 4132.

CHUI, M., P. Levine, M. Murshed and J. Pearlman (February 1998), "Globalisation: A New Growth, New Trade Perspective", Vol. 22, No. 2, *Economic Outlook,* Centre for Economic Forecasting, London Business School.

COE, D. T. and E. Helpman (May 1995), "International R&D Spillovers", *European Economic Review,* Vol. 39, No. 5, pp 859-87.

COLLINS, S. M. and B. P. Bosworth (1996), "Economic Growth in East Asia: Accumulation versus Assimilation", Brookings Papers on Economic Activity, Vol. 2.

CORSETTI, G, P. Pesenti and N.Roubini (1998), What Caused the Asian Currency and Financial Crisis ?, Banca d'Italia, Working Paper Number 343, December 1998.

DEININGER, Klaus and Lyn Squire (1996), "A New Data Set Measuring Income Inequality", *World Bank Economic Review*, Volume 10, No. 3, pp 565-91.

DURLAFS and D. Quah (1998), "The New Empirics of Economic Growth". NBER Working Paper No. 6422.

EDWARDS, S. (April 1995), "Why Are Saving Rates So Different Across Countries? An International Comparative Analysis", NBER Working Paper No. 5097.

EDWARDS, S. (1997a), "Openness, Productivity and Growth: What Do We Really Know?", NBER Working Paper No. 5978.

EDWARDS, S. (1997b), "Trade Policy, Growth and Income Distribution", Papers and Proceedings of the 109th Annual Meeting of the American Economic Association, New Orleans, L.A., January 4-6, 1997, *The American Economic Review*, Vol.87, No.2, pp 205-10.

FISCHER, S (1996), "Lessons from East Asia and the Pacific Rim", Brookings Papers on Economic Activity, Vol. 2.

FRANKEL, J. and Andrew K. Rose. 1996. "Currency Crashes in Emerging Markets: An Empirical Treatment." Journal of International Economics Vol. 41, No.3-4, pp 351-66.

FRY, M (1993), Foreign Direct Investment in Southeast Asia: Differential Impacts, Institute of Southeast Asian Studies, Singapore.

GALLUP, John Luke, Steven Radelet, Andrew Warner (1998), *Economic Growth and the Income of the Poor*, Harvard Institute for International Development.

HELPMAN, E. (1998), "The Structure of Foreign Trade", NBER Working Paper No. 6752.

IMF (1998b), *World Economic Outlook and International Capital Markets, December.*

IMF (1999a), *World Economic Outlook, April*

IMF (1999b), Integrating the Least Developed Countries into the International Trading System, presentation to the WTO High Level Symposium on Trade and Development

KRUEGER, A. O. (1997), "Trade Policy and Economic Development: How We Learn", Vol. 87, No. 1, *The American Economic Review.*

KRUGMAN, P. (1995), "Growing World Trade: Causes and Consequences", Brookings Papers on Economic Activity, Vol. 1.

LAL, D. and H. Myint (1996), *The Political Economy of Poverty, Equity, and Growth, A Comparative Study,* Clarendon Press, Oxford.

LINCOLN, E. J. (1996), "Some Missing Elements", Brookings Papers on Economic Activity, Vol. 2, pp 351-55.

LOW, P., M. Olarreaga and J. Suarez (August 1998), "Does Globalisation Cause a Higher Concentration of International Trade and Investment Flows?", Economic Research and Analysis Division, World Trade Organisation.

MANKIW, N.G. (1995), "The Growth of Nations", Brookings Papers on Economic Activity, Vol. 1, pp 275-310.

McKINNON, R. I and H. Pill (January 1997), "Economic Development and International Trade: Credible Economic Liberalisations and Overborrowing", Papers and Proceedings of the 109th Annual Meeting of the American Economic Association, New Orleans LA, January 4-6 1997, The American Economic Review, May 1997.

MONOD, J. (1997), "Global Integration: The Role of The Private Sector in Promoting Infrastructure Development in Emerging Economies", Keynote Speech at the 1997 Annual Meetings of the World Bank Group and International Monetary Fund.

MORAN, T.H. (1998), Foreign Direct Investment and Development: The New Policy Agenda for Developing Countries and Economies in Transition, Institute for International Economics, Washington.

NADIRI, I. (1993), "Innovations and Technological Spillovers", NBER Working Paper No. 4423.

NELSON, R. (1997), "How New is New Growth Theory?", Challenge, Vol. 40, No. 5, September/October, pp 29-58.

NELSON, R. and H. Pack (1997), "The Asian Miracle and Modern Growth Theory", mimeo, World Bank.

OLSON, M., Jr. (1997), "The Case for Liberalising Markets" (Interview), *Challenge*, Vol. 40, No. 5, September-October, pp 59-76.

PARK, Y. C (1996), "East Asian Liberalisation and the Challenge from China", Brookings Papers on Economic Activity, Vol.2, pp 357-71.

PINHEIRO, João de Deus (1998), *Development Partnership Agreement with the ACP Countries,* EC Commission, DG 8, 30 September 1998.

RODRIK, D. (1996), "Understanding Economic Policy Reform", Vol. 34, No. 1, *Journal of Economic Literature*, Vol.34, No.1, March, pp 9-41.

RODRIK, D. (1998), "Globalisation, Social Conflict and Economic Growth", *The World Economy*, Vol 21, No2, March pp 143-58.

RODRIK, D. (1999), "The New Global Economy and Developing Countries: Making Openness Work". *Policy Essay No. 24.* Overseas Development Council, Washington.

ROEMER, M. (1996), "Could Asian Policies Propel African Growth?", Policy Research Paper, Harvard Institute of International Development.

ROEMER, M. and M.K. Gugerty (1997), "Does Economic Growth Reduce Poverty?", Discussion Paper No. 4, Consulting Assistance on Economic Reform II Harvard Institute of International Development.

SACHS, J. (1995), "Alternative Approaches to Financial Crises in Emerging Markets", Discussion Paper for the Basel meetings, SZ, December 9-10, 1995.

SACHS, J. and S. Radelet (1997), "Asia's Reemergence", *Foreign Affairs,* Volume 76, No. 6, pp 44-59.

SACHS, J. and A. Warner (1995), "Economic Reform and the Process of Global Integration", Brookings Papers on Economic Activity, Vol.1, pp 1-95.

SACHS, J. and A. M. Warner (1997a), "Fundamental Sources of Long-Run Growth", *The American Economic Review*, Vol. 87, No.2, May, pp 184-88.

SACHS, J. and A. M. Warner (1997b), "Sources of Slow Growth in African Economies", *Journal of African Economies,* Vol. 6, No. 3, October, pp 335-76.

SACHS, J. and N. Bajpai (1998), "Strengthening India's Strategy for Economic Growth", Development Discussion Paper No. 641, Harvard Institute for International Development, Harvard University.

SACHS, J. and S. Radelet (1998), "The Onset of the East Asian Financial Crisis", NBER Working Paper No. 6680.

SAFADI, Raed and Sam Laird (1996), "The Uruguay Round and Developing Countries", *Journal of World Development*, Vol. 24, No. 7, July 1996.

SCHMIEG, Evita (1997), *"Coherence between Development Policy and Agricultural Policy"*, Intereconomics, Vol. 32, No.1, January/February, pp 35-40.

SCHON, D.A. (1994) "Hirschman's Elusive Theory of Social Learning", in RODWIN, L. and D. A. Schon ed. (1994), *Rethinking the Development Experience,* Brookings /Lincoln.

SRINIVASAN (1988), Developing Countries and the Multilateral Trading System, Westview Press.

STIGLITZ, J E. (1998), "Towards a New Paradigm for Development: Strategies, Policies and Processes", 1998 Prebisch Lecture at UNCTAD, Geneva, 19 October 1998.

STRYKER, J. D. and S. Pandolfi (1997), "Impact of Outward-Looking, Market-Oriented Policy Reform on Economic Growth and Poverty", Discussion Paper No. 7, Consulting Assistance on Economic Reform II, Harvard Institute of International Development.

TAKATOTSHI, I. (1996), "Japan and the Asian Economies: A 'Miracle' in Transition", Brookings Papers on Economic Activity, Vol. 2, May, pp 205-60.

UNCTAD (1997), *Trade and Development Report.*

UNCTAD (1998), *Trade and Development Report.*

UNCTAD (1999), *Foreign Direct Investment and Development.*

U.S. AGENCY FOR INTERNATIONAL DEVELOPMENT (1998a), "The Development Record and the Effectiveness of Foreign Aid", Bureau for Policy and Program Coordination.

U.S. AGENCY FOR INTERNATIONAL DEVELOPMENT (1998a), "Gaining Ground: World Well-Being 1950-1995", USAID Evaluation Special Study No. 79.

VOS, R. (June 1998), Aid Flows in the Era of Unstable Financial Markets and Volatile Capital Flows, Institute of Social Studies, The Hague, The Netherlands.

WADE, R. (1990), *Governing the Market: Economic Theory and the Role of Government in East Asian Industrialisation,* Princeton University Press.

WORLD BANK (1993), *The East Asian Miracle, Economic Growth and Public Policy,* Oxford University Press.

WORLD BANK, *1998/99 World Development Report,* subtitled "Knowledge for Development", Oxford University Press.

WORLD BANK (1999), A Proposal for a Comprehensive Development Framework, Discussion Draft.

WORLD TRADE ORGANIZATION (1996a), "Participation of Developing Countries in World Trade: Overview of Major Trends and Underlying Factors".

WORLD TRADE ORGANIZATION (1996b), *Annual Report.* Special Topic: Trade and Foreign Direct Investment.

WORLD TRADE ORGANISATION (1998a), *Annual Report.* Special Topic: Globalisation and Trade.

WORLD TRADE ORGANIZATION (1998b), "A Multilateral Agreement on Investment: Convincing the Sceptics". Staff Working Paper, ERAD-98-05.

WORLD TRADE ORGANIZATION (1998c), "Financial Services Trade, Capital Flows, and Financial Stability", Staff Working Paper ERAD-98-12.

ZARSKY, Lyuba (forthcoming 1999), "Havens, Halos and Spaghetti: Untangling the Evidence About Foreign Direct Investment and the Environment". Paper prepared for an OECD Conference on Foreign Direct Investment and Environment, The Hague.

OECD PUBLICATIONS, 2, rue André-Pascal, 75775 PARIS CEDEX 16
PRINTED IN FRANCE
(22 1999 01 1 P) ISBN 92-64-17111-8 – No. 50825 1999